It's

Preparation

Time!

An Informative Guide Before, During, and After
a Time of Transition

Minister Cheryl Hall McElroy

This book is lovingly dedicated in memory to my awesome, wonderful, gentle, sweet Mother, Betty Jane Collins Stanton who was my biggest fan. She went home to be with the Lord on November 25, 2017.

Oh, how I miss your sweet face and funny comments.
8/5/26-11/25/17

Acknowledgements

I would like to acknowledge and dedicate this book to my wonderful and supportive husband, Raleigh C. McElroy, Sr., my children, Chona, Arlondo, Sumer & bonus son, Terance, Jr. and their spouses. I thank God for my Pastor, Overseer Ontiwaun Carter and congregation, of International Restorer of the Breach Ministries, Las Vegas, NV, who entrusted me to create and lead the Ministry of Sick and Bereavement, train our ministers and assist various congregational members during their time of need.

Thank you, Lord for creating me to serve You and Your children. Thank you to every patient, their families, congregants, family & friends, who permitted me to assist you and your family at your time of need when you dealt with the loss of a loved one or allowed me to bring comfort through song, word or deed. Thank you to all who encouraged me to write this book. There are too many to name individually, but know that I love you and appreciate you. Thank you, St. Rose Dominican Hospital's in Las Vegas, NV and Henderson, NV for offering me a position as Hospital Chaplain after I completed my studies and clinicals at your hospitals. I am forever grateful to each of you.

I pray this book will be a blessing to each of you and you will recommend it to family, friends, co-workers, businesses, pastors, ministries or bless them with a copy. I pray God will place this book in every person's hands all over the world as they realize **"It's Preparation Time!"**

To God Be The Glory,

Minister/Chaplain Cheryl Hall McElroy

"I will give thanks to you, Lord, with all my heart; I will tell of all your wonderful deeds."

-Psalm 9:1

Table of Contents

INTRODUCTION

Psalm 23:4 *Yea, though I walk through the valley of the shadow of death, I will fear no evil; for thou art with me; thy rod and thy staff they comfort me.*

I wrote this book to prayerfully help my readers help their families through one of the most difficult times of their lives, and to help them know what to do when the death of a loved one occurs and/or help your family when your death occurs. I know this is not something any of us want to discuss. Some feel as if it is taboo to even bring up the topic of death and/or transitioning. Others feel they're too young to have this discussion. Others feel it's too soon to discuss death because they're not planning on dying any time soon and that they have plenty of time. It's not like we are going to gather our family together and sit at the dining room table or kitchen table and ask each person their wishes when they die and write them down. Yet, it is a very important discussion we all should have with our families before it's too late because tomorrow is not promised.

Hebrews 9:27 KJV says, "And it is appointed unto men once to die, but after this the judgment." Most of us try to put off this appointment as long as possible. But it will happen. These appointments come in various ways—sometimes expected and many times unexpected. By expected I mean, a loved one has a terminal illness and or is in hospice. By unexpected I mean he/she is killed in an accident or has a sudden death.

I remember my first encounter with an unexpected illness. My former husband found a lump in his armpit. He endured many tests to find out what it was. Later, we were told he had cancer, Hodgkin's Disease which is a cancer of the Lymph nodes and Lymph glands and he was also told once he started chemotherapy, we would not be able to conceive if I weren't pregnant already.

We prayed and we had hope so I continued to take a urine test for weeks to see if it would be positive and it wasn't. He had to start chemotherapy and I had to explain to our 2 children that Daddy was sick and we needed to pray for him. My husband and I gave God praise for the 2 beautiful healthy children we had. During chemo, he had to take off from work because of the nausea and I took off to take him to the doctor and care for him after treatment. Bills were beginning to add up. One day I wasn't feeling well and went to my doctor only to find out, "we were pregnant". Look at God! I eventually gave birth to a 9lb. 9oz. healthy baby girl and named her Sumer!

Two years later, my husband succumbed to death. It was such a shock to me and my 2 older children and our families. Our son, Arlondo was in such shock he felt a need to attend school the very next day. I remember him not crying initially but he recently told me he didn't break down and cry for 3 weeks, closer to Thanksgiving. This I didn't remember. Him telling me this still breaks my heart. It was a devasting time for all of us. Our oldest daughter Chona whom her Dad called Squirt, was also in shock and cried often. To lose someone so close to you is devastating and for a child to lose his/her parent in this case at such a young age was painful. My babies had never dealt with a death before. This was their first and it was their Daddy. From this, I learned that everyone deals with grief differently. The important thing is to pray, love, hold, and support them through it. I will speak more on this in a later chapter.

A wonderful hospital chaplain helped me through the most unexpected and difficult times in my life, and it changed my life forever! The comfort, love, peace, prayer, and sincere care I received was phenomenal and I knew in my spirit I wanted to become a Licensed Hospital Chaplain. It is truly a blessing to bring comfort, encouragement, support and prayer to families. Upon completion of reading this guidebook and completing the forms I created, my prayer is that it will help lighten your burden. **It's Preparation Time!**

As I reflect back over my experiences and my desire to write this book, I feel compelled to note that I love hospital ministry. It is truly my calling. I love encouraging people/families, praying for and bringing comfort to those whose loved one is seriously ill, transitioning to go home to be with the Lord or has expired. I was a Per diem Hospital Chaplain on call. We all know it is inevitable, that we all will die. But most of us do not have our stuff in order, we are not "prepared" with the proper legal documents to assist our family at the time of need, serious illness, lengthy hospitalization, or rehab. I have seen so many families divided, torn apart, left with ill feelings towards one another, separated and even divorced after the death of a loved one for one reason or another.

Perhaps they didn't have a Will, Trust or Healthcare Power of Attorney, etc. There was no letter sharing their desires when they died.

Their driver's license or identification did not indicate if they wanted to be an Organ Donor, but someone in the family must decide if they wanted to be or didn't want to be. They had no clue on what to do after a death. What do I do first? Who do I contact? What would my loved one want? Would they want to be cremated or buried? Would they want a viewing or closed casket service? Who is their choice to eulogize them? Would they want their service in a funeral home, church or graveside? Were they a member of the armed service? Where are the documents to support this? What denomination is the loved one? What is their history? I experienced this first hand. I want to share with the world the importance of being as prepared as you can for the inevitable—death. What do I mean by "being prepared"? I'm glad that you asked.

We prepare or save for someone's college education, weddings, honeymoons, home purchase, car purchase, vacation, boat and so much more, but we seldom think that we should purchase a life insurance policy and seek advice from an estate planning & probate attorney. After, experiencing several deaths in my family, bringing comfort and assisting families as a Hospital Chaplain and minister and woman of God, I present to you the book, **"It's Preparation Time! An Informative Guide Before, During and After a Time of Transition."**

Why This Book and Why Now? | 1

"Do not boast about tomorrow, for you do not know what a day may bring forth."
Proverbs 27:1 (NIV)

On January 17, 2017, I wrote the following Facebook post:

LETTER TO FAMILY ABOUT MY MOTHER

To my family and friends: Mom/Granny/Aunt Betty/Ms. Betty/Sis. Stanton is doing as well as could be expected in the last stage of Alzheimer's with the assistance of Hospice. I am thanking God for "Preparation time". We know Alzheimer's usually ends in death. On average, a person with Alzheimer's lives four to eight years after diagnosis, but can live as long as 20 years, depending on other factors. This is from my heart and it's long. You don't have to read it nor respond.

Sometimes death is sudden, expected, prolonged or accidental. Mom's is prolonged which for me is "Preparation Time". Sometimes God grants us "Preparation Time" to get our stuff together. In other words, God could have snatched Mom from this life a long time ago. But in His infinite wisdom He permitted Mom to live 91 years and the last 7 with Alzheimer's.

Because of her diagnosis, we could still enjoy her and also watch her as she aged and declined. It wasn't easy. Even though one can never be completely ready for a death, God can allow you time to get your documents/Funeral plans together ahead of time. Even though you think you're ready, you're not.

From there, I proceeded to tell my FB family that, God blessed my husband and I with 7 years of caring for Mom. I want you to know why I love my Mom so much and post as much as I do about her on a daily basis. Many years ago, Mom had a will, Power of Attorney and Healthcare Power of Attorney, etc. completed and named me to make decisions for her when she couldn't. When I suspected my Mother, Betty Collins Stanton could possibly have dementia and lived alone as a widow, in my hometown of Indianapolis, IN, my husband, my Mother and I agreed to move her to Nevada with us because she needed 24-hour care. Since Raleigh was and is retired and I worked 3 days a week, it worked out perfectly for us to move her here—just the 3 of us! I sought legal counsel and became my mom's legal guardian.

Raleigh loves my Mother and she loves him. She affectionately calls him, "handsome", because he is to us. Many of our church members thought my husband was my mother's son because they were always together when he brought her to bible study and church. He brought her because as a Minister I had to arrive earlier, so we drove separately. But not only that, he truly loved Mom and she loved him like her son. He took Mom to the casino (mom called it "casina"…lol) on a daily basis to play slots and/or bingo. She loved it! He also took her to lunch or dinner at times. They were road dogs. The code word for taking

Mom to the "casina" lol, when she got agitated, was "Hey Mom, wanna get some fresh air?" That meant "wanna go to the casina?" She would laugh and say, "let me get my shoes on" and off they went.

Understand, there was family in Indianapolis and other cities who would love to have cared for Mom but couldn't due to fulltime jobs and caring for their families. Our families live in various cities & states which is why my children had me post on Facebook and Instagram to keep everyone abreast of how Mom was doing. Mom lived with us for 5 1/2 years before we placed her in Memory Care 2 1/2 years ago. We decided if Mom ever got out of the house on her own, we would place her in a Memory Care facility.

One night about 2:30 a.m., I was awakened by the chime on the door. I jumped up to find Mom's bed made and she was not in the house. I ran out the front door and saw Mom completely dressed walking across the street. I yelled "Mom, she kept walking. I yelled "Betty" as I ran toward her. She stopped, turned around smiling at me and said, "how did you find me? I calmly said, "Mom where are you going? She said I'm going to see my niece where the porch light is on. I said, she's not at home right now, let's go back to bed and you can visit her tomorrow. She said ok. What I did is called "Redirection". It is a technique in which you shift a distressed person's attention away from the situation causing anger, anxiety, fear, or dangerous or unsafe behavior.

Mom was an awesome cook and baker. Well known for her fried chicken, greens, homemade rolls, checkerboard cakes, sweet potato pies and so much more! She babysat (ole school Day Nursery) black and white children for over 55 years. She actually kept 3 and 4 generations of families.

My mother never met a stranger and welcomed all into her home and made you sit down and eat or take a plate. She fed the children she cared for 3-4 course homemade meals, 3 times a day plus snacks, bathed them, combed their hair, potty trained them, made them take naps, kept them clean, cared for them when they had bad colds or weren't feeling well so their parents could go to work; she loved them as her own. We would sometimes laugh and say that Mom reminded us of the popular nursery rhyme, "the old woman who lived in a shoe who had so many children, she didn't know what to do."

So I vowed that every day as long as Mom is here with us, I would continue to share via social media with our family and friends how Mom/Granny/Aunt Betty is doing.

After Mom got out of the house, I began searching for Memory Care facilities. Please do your homework. Go inside the facility, talk to staff. I chose a lovely group home that had 10 patients and I thought it was very nice and clean; the staff was very nice and professional. It was very hard to take Mom and leave her. I had to trick her to get her in there then run out the door. I cried a river of tears and asked God to help me. I couldn't see her in person for a month, but I was there every day checking on her. The staff would sneak me in through the garage so I could peek at her while she was eating or watching television. I cried. I wanted to hug and kiss her so bad, but I couldn't because she had to get use to the facility and staff. But Mom became a piece of work. Sometimes when I called to check on her to see how she was doing, the staff said Mom would yell at them to let her out; she wanted to go home so she pulled on the door handles to get out. She knocked on the windows and hollered, "help me, get me out of here" or she would cuss at them and threaten to call the police on them. Eventually, she calmed down with the help of medication and I was able to see her sweet, beautiful face and kiss her soft cheeks. We were so happy to see one another. I asked her how she liked her "new apartment?" She said, "it's fine." She was in there 3 months and developed a bedsore! I was very distraught to say the least and removed her and placed her in a larger Memory Care facility. She was there 2 years until she went home to be with the Lord with family surrounding her.

My mother's story is uniquely ours, but I am sure there are many of you who are reading this book now who can relate. You have served as a care giver, a doting child, spouse, parent, grandmother, sister or friend during a time of need, sickness, and illness. Whatever the role, when we encounter death, regardless of the circumstance, it is not easy. In fact, it may be one of the most difficult things that we ever encounter.

This chapter is intended to provide you with a space to exhale, to take a deep breath, sigh, cry out or even moan—you are not alone. What you are experiencing is perfectly okay and your process of preparing for death is perfectly ok.

As I write this book, I think about my mom and I think about all of the families that I have ministered to throughout the years. I have been doing hospital ministry for 36 years. I have been a Licensed Hospital Chaplain for 15 years and an Ordained Minister for 20 years. I have spent many hours ministering to families, praying with them, comforting them, encouraging them and loving on them. I thank God for this "calling" because everyone can't do this and has not been called to this office of Chaplaincy or Minister. I love God and I trust Him, but this, hurts. It's my Mother who is and has been my best friend, my confidant, my girlfriend, my road dog, my shoulder to cry on, my counselor/advisor, my prayer warrior and now she is about to transition to heaven. Yes, I have moments when I cry, because I see her not eating and losing weight, and becoming lethargic etc. I listen as her long-term memory kicks in, sometimes not knowing who we are, talking about her deceased family members who stopped by to see her and how she wants to go home.

She calls me Moma/Mother & calls Raleigh Daddy/Father. Yes, I/we will miss my/our Mother. We will miss her presence, her smile, her kisses that she called "sugars", her cussing, yes, Moma wrote the book on profanity. She even made up her own cuss words. I'll miss her laughter, cooking, dancing, yes Moma was a dancer, she could do the "dog" which is getting on her hands and knees and shaking her rear end. Some of y'all are too young to remember that, but my Mother enjoyed life to the fullest and for that I am thankful.

I rejoice and celebrate my Mother's life because God promised her threescore and ten (70) Psalm 90:10 but He graced her with an additional 21 years. I say that because we laugh sometimes saying Mom will probably outlive all of us. Mom has been saved a long time and when God decides to call her home, it is well with my soul. I asked God to not let her suffer or be in pain and He said to me, "My Grace is sufficient" 2 Corinthians 12:9, and I believe Him and His Word. I am so grateful God put Raleigh and I in position to care for Mom.

When we got married 20 years ago, my husband and I agreed if our parents became ill, we would take care of them no matter what, until God called them home. We are thankful that we were able to honor this. Similarly, we know that you will experience great comfort and peace in knowing what your loved one desires and your role in making sure that those desires are fulfilled.

Readers, tomorrow is not promised to any of us. The Word of God says in Heb. 9:27 KJV "And as it is appointed unto men once to die, but after this the judgment." We all are going to die. We don't know how, when or where. We don't know the day nor the hour. Everybody wants to go to heaven, but nobody wants to die. If you can, put all your hurt in the past and love and care for your parents, children/loved ones while you can. My husband says all the time: "Live each day as though it's your last and you will have few regrets." I can honestly say Raleigh and I have no regrets because we did the best we could in loving and caring for Mom.

During this time of transition, (the process or a period of changing from one state or condition to another), I posted pictures so our family and friends could stay abreast of what is going on with their Mother, Grandmother, Aunt, Cousin and friend. For you, you may listen to your loved one's favorite music, listen to his/her favorite song or even revisit a place that is anchored in fond memories. During the time of transition, we all embrace our loved one in different ways. If you are the primary care giver, you may also want to share this deeply personal time with others who aren't nearby.

My mom helped raise almost all of her nieces and nephews and they loved her as she loved them. This may mirror your family which is why you should take advantage of preparation time by enjoying every moment you can with your loved one. Go see them, spend time with them, love them if you can or call them. If you need to forgive, do it and love them. Matthew 6:14-15 KJV "For if ye forgive men their trespasses, your heavenly Father will also forgive you: But if ye forgive not men their trespasses, neither will your Father forgive your trespasses." That's what Jesus has done for you and me. I am not sad; I celebrate and honor my Mother daily. Rejoice with your love one and take advantage of God's season of transition.

Sometimes, it is only in hindsight that we see the gift. Today is just that—a gift. A gift that allows us to prepare for what's to come. Some of this will be familiar; yet, other aspects of this season will be foreign and unfamiliar. As a clinician, my advice to you is to understand that our deaths are inevitable. Don't wait until your loved one, or even you, are diagnosed with a serious or terminal illness or an accident occurs for you to spend quality time with the people you care deeply about, loving them and making lifelong memories.

I strongly encourage you to take several steps that will make the process smoother for you. For example, you should purchase life insurance, seek professional counsel regarding estate planning, create a living will, write a trust, etc. Place these important items in a safe and secure place. Most importantly, find out the wishes of your loved one and write them down on the forms I provide for you in the last chapter of this book.

The hardest part is making sure that you do all of the aforementioned for "yourself". It may not be easy to think about your own transition, but it will help your loved ones. Furthermore, tell your loved one(s) where this pertinent information can be found. You will be surprised how doing this will lighten the burden when someone transitions and how much it will help your family when you transition. Enjoy life by living each day as though it's your last and you will have few regrets and a lifetime of love. You will also give your family the gift of being prepared.

As we prepare for the next chapter, do know that this book was inspired by God. He placed it on my heart to put in writing and to share with you what I have been doing for over 36 years and that is: giving comfort to those whose family members are about to transition, assisting people with funerals by doing the hair and makeup for their deceased loved one, assisting with writing the obituary, creating the program for the funeral or memorial service, singing, being the M.C., reading condolences, reading the obituary, conducting the eulogy, counseling, or just bringing comfort through prayer, hugs, and encouraging words before their loved one expires and/or after they expire. And now you can prepare your loved one's program/obituary. It is my desire that the words and resources that I share in this book will bless you during your preparation process.

"All scripture is God-breathed and is useful for teaching, rebuking, correcting and training in righteousness."

-2 Timothy 3:16 NIV

Preparing for the Transition Phase | 2

"There is a time for everything and a season, for every activity under heavens: a time to be born and a time to die."
Ecclesiastes 3:1-2 (NIV)

If you are reading this book that means either you have lost a loved one, a loved one is about to pass, or you are taking the necessary precautionary actions to prepare and list your desires before death occurs. When we lose a loved one, the pain we experience can feel unbearable. I feel your pain and as you'll read, several of my loved ones have transitioned. Through my grief and pain, I learned a lot and prayerfully by sharing, it will lessen your burden.

Grieving is a uniquely individual process. No two people grieve the same. Don't let anyone tell you what's supposedly "normal" or the "best" way to grieve. Grief is deep sorrow especially when it is caused by death.

Synonyms: sorrow, misery, sadness, anguish, pain, distress, agony torment, affliction, suffering, heartache, heartbreak, broken heartedness, heaviness of heart, woe, desolation, despondency, dejection, despair, angst, mortification and so much more.

Some people find that grief is like swimming in the ocean. It comes in waves. One minute you feel fine, then the next, you seem to be drowning in tears. Go with the flow. Ride the waves and try not to resist them. It's ok to cry. It's ok to be angry, just don't stay there. The following are the five stages of grief:

1. Denial
2. Anger
3. Bargaining
4. Depression
5. Acceptance

The 5 stages of grief were first proposed by Elisabeth Kubler-Ross in her 1969 book *On Death and Dying*. The stages of grief and mourning are universal and are experienced by people from all walks of life, across many cultures. Mourning occurs in response to an individual's own terminal illness, the loss of a close relationship, or to the death of a valued being, human or animal. Keep in mind that not everyone will experience these stages in the exact same order or in the same way. Also, some people may spend more time in one stage than the other.

In our bereavement, we spend different lengths of time working through each step and express each stage with different levels of intensity. The key to understanding the stages is not to feel like you must go through every stage. Instead, it's more helpful to look at them as guides in the grieving process. They can help you understand and put into context where you are. We often move between stages before achieving a more peaceful acceptance of someone's death.

All are a part of the framework that makes up our ability to live without the one who has died. They are tools to help us frame and identify what we may be feeling. But they are not a rigid, linear timeline for grief. In other words, there is not a prescribed order. Instead, my hope is that these stages will lead to greater knowledge about grief's terrain, making us better equipped to cope with life and death. At times, people in grief will often report more than these stages. Just remember, your grief is as unique as you are.

The death of your loved one might inspire you to evaluate your own feelings of mortality. Prayerfully, it will encourage you to prepare. Throughout each stage, a common thread of hope emerges. As long as there is life, there is hope. As long as there is hope, there is life.

I urge you to explore all the emotions your grief raises including relief, if that applies. I also urge you to obtain all the emotional and spiritual support you need from friends, family, clergy and perhaps a grief counselor, licensed therapist and/or a support group. I also urge you to read some of the many books that have been written about grieving. Because of this, I recommend that everyone, regardless of age, read books that will help them prepare for death or the transition of a loved one.

The truth is that death is inevitable. It is going to happen, but often we are not prepared. When that time comes to support someone you love, do you know what to do? I would venture to say no.

Do you have a life insurance policy that will pay for your funeral expenses? Do you have enough insurance to make sure that your family is well provided for? Or will you have to sell chicken dinners, fish dinners, ask family and/or friends to help, get a pay day loan or create a Go Fund Me page to pay for the all expenses for the loved one's funeral or "your funeral".

I know firsthand why this is so important. I became a widow at the age of 29 when my first husband passed away from Hodgkin's Disease. He was 30 years old and we had three beautiful children ages 11, 8 and 2. As I mentioned previously, we were told if I wasn't pregnant before he started chemotherapy, we would not be able to conceive because chemo would kill his sperm. I said to the doctor "the devil is a liar in Jesus name".

I believed in my heart I would get pregnant because my husband and I touched and agreed in prayer that I would conceive. After several weeks of taking my urine to the lab to see if I was pregnant before he started chemotherapy, I was not. We finally accepted I was not pregnant, but I never stopped praying and believing. Because God can do anything except fail, we continued to believe with great fervent and faith. As he started chemotherapy, we were grateful and gave God praise for our 2 healthy children whom we loved and continued on with life.

Around that same time, I remember that I needed to have foot surgery, but I put it off since we were trying to get pregnant. Since I was not pregnant and my husband had started chemo, I opted to have the foot surgery. A month or so later after I had the foot surgery, my husband went with me to my next doctor's appointment. While there, they did routine bloodwork and told us that we were pregnant! We were ecstatic! All I could do was cry happy tears and give God the Glory! We called her our "miracle baby". Genesis 50:20 says: "You intended to harm me, but God intended it for good to accomplish what is now being done, the saving of many lives." I could hardly wait to tell our family. God did that! We prayed and believed God for a healthy baby and he answered our prayers.

Next, I saw my OBGYN. When I told him I recently had foot surgery, he said I should consider having an abortion because I had been under general anesthesia for the foot surgery and that there would be a risk of the baby having congenital anomalies at birth, a lower birth rate or other more challenging possibilities and deformities.

Once again, I said, "the devil is a liar". We prayed about it and decided if God allowed me to get pregnant knowing I had been under anesthesia then he would take care of me and allow me to give birth to a healthy baby. Well he did just that. God blessed us with a 9lb. 9oz., 21 inches long, healthy baby girl. And my husbands' cancer was in remission. We gave God all the Praise Honor and Glory!

It was also around this time that we had lived in a rented townhouse for almost five years and decided to start saving to buy our first home. In the process, we started to eliminate as much debt as we possibly could. In the midst of paying off some of our bills to lower our debt to income ratio to purchase a new home, my husband decided to drop one of his personal life insurance policies that we had on him because the payment was high. Although I disagreed with his doing this, I also understood why he did it since he had a small policy through his job. Sadly, he believed he could get another policy later. I kept telling him, no we won't be able to get another policy because he had been diagnosed with cancer. Or if we did get one, it would be very expensive. One year later, 1981 God blessed us to build and move into our first new five-bedroom home. I was 28 and he was 29. We were so excited and grateful to God for this blessing. A year after moving into our new home, the cancer returned. I remember my husband saying to me one evening after the cancer returned that we needed to sit down and have a serious conversation. I remember it as though it was yesterday.

We sat at our dining room table and he said I know we only have a small insurance policy but please do all you can to keep this house. I interrupted him, saying "I don't want to hear this, you will be fine and we will live in this house forever." He said, "honey, listen please. I want you and our children to remain in this house we built for them if at all possible." With tears streaming down my cheeks, I said, "ok" as we held each other close. He felt he needed to prepare me because we both knew that with the cancer returning, tomorrow was not promised for him.

Almost exactly, one year later, my husband passed away on November 2, 1982. I truly thank God that he gave us time to prepare before it was too late. I began to thank God and count all of the blessings He blessed us with. God could have taken my husband instantly, but He allowed me and our families to spend quality time loving him and enjoying him. He blessed us to get pregnant when odds were against us according to the OBGYN. God also allowed my husband to be in the delivery room with me to witness our daughter's birth though he almost passed out. God blessed us to build our first home and to have him live in and decorate the family room (his mancave) for a year. He was a licensed electrician for his job. Our nice five-bedroom bi-level home was beautiful. The lower level was unfinished and he and our cousin Phillip (R.I.H.) finished the lower level before he passed away. He was so proud of his accomplishments and so was I. Me and our children lived in that home for 13 years, until I decided to sell it and move to another home. That was nothing but God! He does answer prayer!

Losing a loved one is an experience we all know we will have to deal with, but most of us are not ready emotionally, physically, or financially ready. I was told this is something you cannot prepare for. I beg to differ. If you purchase a life insurance policy that will at least cover the funeral expenses and if you write down your desires as far as funeral service and after care expenses then that will help out also.

But we don't because we don't want to talk about it. Yes, it is a hard conversation to have, but it is needed. Or we feel we have plenty of time and will take care of it "tomorrow or later." But sometimes later comes sooner than we think. It just so happened that the small life insurance policy my husband had through his job did pay for his funeral, thank God. But what if we didn't have a policy at all and no savings.

Unfortunately, attending widow support groups opened my eyes to the frequency in which spouses are not prepared. I was the youngest widow in the group. They brought in various speakers to share suggestions on grief and how to continue living after a death.

So many people gave encouragement but what truly helped me was my faith in God, my children, my friends and family who were by my side every step of the way. Yes, I had difficult days and somedays it seemed as if I cried a river of tears. I missed him so much. Our baby was 2 years old when her Daddy died. She often asked for him. There were days I didn't want to do anything or go anywhere, but my faith in

God and my babies gave me reason, strength and love to make it every day. It wasn't easy, but God!

There are many decisions that must be made after a death that I will expound upon later in this book. One very important thing I want to share is "do not make any major decisions 6 months to a year or more after losing a spouse or someone very close to you" because of the other stressors you're likely also experiencing you may make the wrong decision. For example, you may have to decide if it is best to sell your existing home or purchase a new home. Packing and actually moving to a new residence generally proves to be a huge undertaking at any time, so be sure not to make a decision that you may later regret.

Remember, you may need extra time.to heal and that is ok. In addition to the fact that you're taxed physically, emotionally, mentally or spiritually following your loss and you've already had to complete many tasks after a loved one's death, moving may not be something you want to do at this point.

This is just one example of something that you may want to wait to do. There are numerous others, including getting remarried, starting a new job, leaving your place of worship or detaching yourself from a support community that truly loves and cares about your well-being.

While it might be tempting to do these things to escape reminders of your deceased loved one, waiting is in your best interest, especially financially. It's entirely possible that you might view your living or financial situation differently after several months or after the settling of your loves one's estate.

So, avoid making a hasty decision if you can. If you've ever acted rashly in an emotional moment by saying or doing something that you later regretted, then you should trust that now is not the time to discard mementos, keepsakes, photographs, and other reminders of your beloved one even if these items trigger sadness and tears while your grief feels the freshest.

Once something is "hauled to the curb" or taken away, these irreplaceable and tangible connections between you and someone you love will be gone forever. It is not as simple as changing your mind and these things will return. Unlike movies where one can rewind, life does not have such a function.

Therefore, you should delay throwing out any items, giving away clothes or jewelry, etc. that are linked to your loved one as you grieve. If you have someone who you can lean on, ask him/her to help you sort and organize the deceased person's belongings. In time, perhaps six months or a year or more you might feel differently as you begin adjusting to life after the loss of your loved one. But if you simply cannot tolerate these physical reminders right now, then consider boxing them up and storing them in a spare room, garage, basement, a friend's house or even a rented storage unit to remove them from your living space.

Despite the suggestions that I have shared, only you know the unique circumstances that you face during the time immediately following the death of your loved one. We all grieve differently and we all deserve to grieve in a way that can bring about healing. Therefore, if delaying a particular life decision for six months to a year doesn't seem feasible, then you should first discuss the situation with a trusted friend or confidant. If you are a person of faith, your spiritual leader is a great resource as well.

If it's a financial decision that you need to make, seek the opinion of a professional financial advisor or wealth management specialist. Sometimes simply having a conversation with someone who has your best interest at heart can help you gain a better sense of perspective. Having a springboard to help you process and reflect can also help you realize that the situation is less urgent than it may feel to you during that particular moment.

Five years after the loss of my first husband, a friend set me up on a blind date. Many friends kept telling me that I needed to start dating since it had been five years. But I was fine, I did think it would be nice to go to a movie or lunch or dinner, but I thought it was too soon to meet someone.

The man I would meet was a customers' brother. She spoke very highly of him; she also told me how much of a gentleman he was and that he was in ministry. That made me feel better, so I agreed to go on a blind date. I was so nervous. We went to a gospel concert. It was great and he was such a kind man of God. We dated long distance for a few months. He was an awesome cook who loved his family and friends. He was also very active in his church.

He supported me when the gospel singing group I sung with engaged in ministerial duties at various locations and events; he also supported me when I was singing solo somewhere. I supported him when he taught bible study or preached. We also sometimes taught as a tag team. It was great. Then he was ready to get married and I wasn't. I felt as if it was too soon for me. We sought counsel from my Bishop/Pastor at that time and we never told him anything prior about the reason for our meeting.

At our meeting, Bishop felt in his spirit that we should not get married at that time. He thought that we should take more time to get to know one another and pray for a year or so. If, at that time, we still felt the same way, then we should revisit the idea of marriage. My friend was hurt but we departed friends and remained friends and prayer partners for several years.

I share this with you because even though it had been seven years since my husband passed away, my emotions were still all over the place and I didn't want to make a mistake and enter into remarriage prematurely. Satan was busy. Trust me: Do not rush into the decision making, especially something that will affect you for many, many years to come. I'm a witness!

A year or so later, I met someone else that was fun, entertaining and in the limelight. We went out dancing; we went to secular concerts, parties etc. I had not danced or had fun like that in "years". I had given my life to Christ and basically only went to church and work. Anyway, even though I saw several red flags before my eyes, when that person proposed, I said 'yes'.

Lord Jesus, what did I do? I re-married. Experiencing something you have not experienced before or in a long time can lead you to make a wrong decision. Some of my friends and family told me I shouldn't marry that person, but I didn't listen. So instead of truly seeking God and waiting on Him, instead of going to God in prayer and waiting on Him, I went on feelings and emotions, I got married when I shouldn't have.

A few days before the wedding and on my wedding day, I felt in my spirit I shouldn't get married to that person, but pride set in. I didn't want to be embarrassed by announcing to families and guests the wedding was off, so I went through with it. If I had to do it over again, that's exactly what I would have done … called it off! A divorce can hurt like a "death".

The difference is with a death, you won't see that person anymore so it's more final. But with divorce you could possibly run into that person again which could bring up the hurt and anger you experienced all over again. I truly had to call on the name of the Lord to help me with that situation. There was hurt, shame, embarrassment, infidelity anger, lack of trust. I felt like a fool.

I knew better but I believed in marriage "til death do you part". I didn't believe in divorce so I stayed longer than I should have. I went through so much hurt in that marriage that I can honestly say I experienced the 5 stages of grief: anger, denial, bargaining, depression and acceptance. I could not stand the way I was feeling. I kept saying, I knew better, and I cried out to God to help me.

Anger was the one emotion that I held onto the longest. I was angry at him, but I was also angry with myself. I had all kinds of signs but believed I should pray, stay and forgive. I had to surrender him and I over to the Lord. It did not happen overnight, but I truly gave it over to God and asked for forgiveness and I forgave my ex-husband. I thank God that one day several years after our divorce we ran into each other and he asked if he could talk to me. Of course, me with the attitude, said "for what?

Anyway, I gave him maybe 5 minutes or less to say what he had to say and he said "I am so sorry for hurting you and treating you the way I did. I'm asking you to forgive me." I accepted his apology, forgave him and moved on with my life as he did his. God is so good and merciful. God is love and God is forgiving. Colossians 3:13 says:

> *Bearing with one another and, if one has a complaint against another, forgiving each other, as the Lord has forgiven you, so you also must forgive.*

God knows His children. He knows we are hardheaded. So, He just sat back and let me have free will to make a huge mistake that "I learned from". Thank you, Lord. So, a year or so later, I was contacted by my "blind date friend" that wanted to marry me. He knew I was divorced and said he had been praying for me. Look at God! Remember that song, "Somebody prayed for me, had me on their mind, took the time to pray for me. I'm so glad they prayed, I'm so glad they prayed, I'm so glad they prayed for me."

Well, I am so grateful and thankful for friends and family that prayed for me—their blind, crippled and crazy sister in Christ. My blind date friend wanted to have lunch or dinner. I told him let's take time to seek God in prayer before seeing one another because I didn't want to hurt him, be hurt or be on the rebound since it hadn't been that long since my divorce.

We agreed to pray individually and together. We had been friends and prayer partners for 10 years, then he proposed. This time I did seek the Lord and waited for His answer of approval before accepting his proposal. Yes, we got married. He was a divorcee of 15 years at the time. We both loved married life and was grateful God finally allowed us to get married. If it could have worked out with our first spouse, we would have remained married to them if God said the same.

One of the beautiful things about my husband is he had taken care of his business, including estate planning. Shortly, after we were married, he took me to sign papers so I would not have to be concerned about anything. I wondered why he did this so quickly and soon I found out.

Shortly after our marriage, my husband told me he had been going to the doctor because he had a bad cold that had lingered for a while. Several tests were given and he was diagnosed with Renal Cell Carcinoma. I asked what that was? He said kidney cancer. My heart skipped a beat. I could not believe that once again, here I was faced with someone I loved facing cancer. Once again, I found myself turning to my faith to help me help my husband through this season of uncertainty.

They did x-rays and found he had pneumonia but also found nodules on his lungs which indicated lung cancer. I told him we are going to pray because God can do anything except fail. So we prayed together immediately. I then asked why he didn't tell me sooner; he said because he knew in his heart it would not matter when he told me, because of the love we shared and what God had told him. He knew

I would take care of him til death do us part like we said in our vows and like I did my first husband and that is exactly what I did. He became Pastor of an AME church, I was ordained, we had a wonderful, small loving congregation.

We enjoyed our lives loving each other and spending time with our family and friends having people over for dinner, playing cards, games, cooking and enjoying Christmas which was his favorite holiday, he loved the snow. When he began to decline, I closed my beauty salon and came home to care for him until he took his last breath in our home. Losing someone you love is "devastating". I was angry at myself for not marrying him when he first asked me because we could have had 10 years together.

But that was not in God's plan. To lose two husbands, oh my gosh! There was a lesson(s) I was to learn from this. I would not wish that on my worst enemy. I experienced so many different emotions, again various stages of grief.

Yes, I was even angry with God. I couldn't understand why He would put me through losing another spouse. Then a small voice said to me, God gives us free will to make choices.

Sometimes we have to hit rock bottom or hit our head several times before we can see the Hand of God or be still long enough to allow Him to speak to us. I was hardheaded and wanted to do things my way. The bible says Ephesians 4:26, (NIV) In your anger do not sin: Do not let the sun go down while you are still angry.

I cried out to God with my every being. Then a peace came over me as it says in Philippians 4:7 (NIV) "And the peace of God, which transcends all understanding, will guard your hearts and your minds in

Christ Jesus." Then one day after prayer, I sat down and was still. I heard God say, "I allowed you to go through losing another spouse because "I knew you could handle it". I know you are my faithful servant daughter that I "trust" and my son could trust you to care for him. My God, the tears flowed, and I shouted, I worshipped and I praised God non-stop.

Then of course there were days the enemy tried to come into my thoughts and try to impart negativity through people saying horrible things, when I put on a CD and that song is what got me through those grieving days: "No Weapon Formed Against Me Shall Prosper" by Fred Hammond.

Even today I truly thank God for prayer, my faith and my life as I have grown stronger in God. I realize that everything that I have endured, even through the grief, allowed me to see the "hands of God" in all of it. I thank God for loving me enough to give me the strength to endure.

I encourage each of you reading this book to open your hearts and let God in to heal your wounds. It may be a song that will bring you through, it could be scripture(s), an encouraging word or hug. It may be a memento or even a favorite place filled with memories.

You may not understand why you're going through what you're going through right now, but God will reveal it in due season. This is where your faith is paramount to your healing. God will anchor you through this very difficult phase.

Driving home one day, I put in Yolonda Adams CD and let it play all the way through when one song, spoke to my heart, "I'm Just A Prayer Away." I cried and sung all the way home. God is so good! I knew God was with me and would help me through this just like He did everything else I went through. God is no respecter of persons; what He did for me He will do for you. The love, fun and friendship my husband and I shared in one- and one-half years of marriage was more than what some couples have that have been married 30 years. He was truly an awesome man of God.

God blessed me to get married again and my current husband Raleigh and I recently celebrated 20 years of marriage on July 10. Once we were married, we too sought an estate planning attorney to get our affairs together and we did. We did this because we wanted to make sure that we did not burden our families with deciding who gets what. It is so important because as you know, tomorrow is not promised. We both had been married before, so we knew the importance of taking care of business immediately. When we became one, we blended our families together.

If you are in a marriage where there are children from previous marriages, you want to make sure that you don't leave your children in a position where there may be fighting, disagreement or even worse—the need to go to probate court.

All of our children are adults and are doing well. I have an awesome husband who was a widower. We are blessed that God placed us in each other's lives when He did. We both have had health challenges, but we, thankfully, take care of one another. He is a fine, handsome, supportive, intelligent man of integrity. He is also a businessman of integrity who loves and cares deeply for me, his wife and our family.

I love him so much and truly thank God for him. He supports my ministry and everything I do in every way. We love making each other happy. Since we both have loss spouses, we realize that tomorrow is not promised so we live each day as though it's our last. We enjoy attending bible study, church, listening to jazz, live music, dancing, playing board games with friends, entertaining and loving our family. In other words, because we have prepared for our future together, there are many things that we can enjoy without worrying about the "what ifs" that some other people have to worry about.

I am writing this book not to gloat, but to, hopefully, help you and others get your business in order as to not put a burden on your family. It is going to be hard enough, so why not put your wishes in writing by using the forms I created and seeking a professional estate planning attorney to have a will or trust created, because it is needed.

As a woman who brings a wealth of information to this discussion—I am a Licensed Cosmetologist of 38 years, Licensed Cosmetology Instructor/Director 16 years, Licensed Ordained Minister 22 years and a Licensed Hospital Chaplain 17 years—I am offering you real world experiences and examples that highlight the importance of looking beyond today and preparing for tomorrow.

I have been a facilitator and I have taught the *Look Good Feel Better* program for the American Cancer Society for over 20 years. I have seen and offered comfort to many families since 1982. After the experience I had after my first husband's death at such a young age,

God placed on my heart to try to help anyone I can with the service of their loved one such as: pray with them, encourage them, visit them and/or their family, offer to go with them to the funeral home when making arrangements, offer comfort, offer to assist with the arrangements, sing at the service, create their program/obituary for the service, bring the words of comfort or eulogy, offer my cosmetology services to do the make-up and/or hair, polish their nails of their loved one to reassure their loved one looks as normal as possible. I assist families in whatever way I am permitted. In doing so, I understand the complexity of death and dying.

We prepare for retirement, we save money to purchase a new home, new car, we save money for our children to go to college or purchase their first car and so much more. We prepare for everything except "death". Hebrews 9:27 (KJV) says: (a clause) And as "it is appointed unto men once to die".

I am writing this book to assist each of my sisters and brothers with suggestions/instructions on how to prepare for your Homegoing or Celebration of Life. Prayerfully this book will provide tools that will make it easier for you and families because you are sharing your wishes in preparing for something that we all know is going to happen, but no one wants to talk about or prepare for and that's death.

"Fear thou not; for I am with thee: be not dismayed; for I am thy God: I will strengthen thee: yea, I will help thee; yea, I will uphold thee with the right hand of my righteousness."

- Isaiah 41:10 KJV

What to Do "Before" Death Occurs | 3

"Let all things be done decently and in order".
1 Corinthians 14:40 (KJV)

I strongly recommend that you seek professional counsel in all areas. It is tempting to just rely upon a friend or maybe someone who we are connected with on social media, but during times such as this, you want to seek the counsel of people who have wisdom, experience, credentials, and the required licensure in their respective fields. One of the first things that you should consider, if you have not already is a life insurance policy.

LIFE INSURANCE

You should consider purchasing a life insurance policy if nothing else, for your funeral cost. Policies are term, whole life (builds cash value), universal, variable, variable universal, simplified issue, guaranteed issue life, final expense insurance and group life insurance.

Be sure to seek advice from a Licensed Insurance agent for your specific needs. You can use life insurance policies to help your loved ones pay for college tuition, mortgage payments and help cover retirement income gaps in the event of your passing. Some Permanent policies offer the opportunity to build cash value, which you're able to use however you like. You will make premium payments each month so in the event of your passing, your loved ones and beneficiaries will receive the death benefit proceeds from the policy. Term insurance is for a specific period of time whereas permanent is for life as long as the premiums are paid. Please do your research, ask questions before settling on a policy. It is also a good idea to get multiple quotes from different companies.

I purchased a Whole Life $10,000 policy for my Mother after my 1st husband passed. She was 56 years of age. My mother lived longer than expected according to the insurance company, so her policy depreciated. I just knew whenever Mom passed away, I would have enough for a decent burial. Well, I didn't. Because of family and friends' generous donations and Go Fund Me, my mom had 2 beautiful Homegoing Celebrations in two different states. PLEASE, do your research, ask questions and get professionals to assist you to accommodate your needs. During your time of need, you want to have time to process and it is better to have more than enough than not enough.

ESTATE PLANNING

Also look into Estate Planning. An Estate plan outlines how you would like to care for the things that are most important to you like your kids, pets, your home, etc. A Will is a plan for who will look after your children and what should happen to your assets, if something happens. A trust will assist in avoiding probate with a complete plan for the protection and transfer of your most important assets.

A trust is more complicated and more expensive to set up and manage than a Will, but, after death, a trust does not have to go through the time-consuming, expensive probate process. The beneficiaries receive their gifts immediately, or according to the trust instructions. The question of whether a Trust or Will is better for you has no simple answer since so many factors must be considered in estate planning. What is right for you might be very wrong for someone else. I am not an attorney. Please seek counsel from a Professional Estate Planning Attorney for advice.

GUARDIANSHIP

(This information was gathered from Matthew G. Pfau, Esq. Parry & Pfau, 880 Seven Hills Dr., Suite 210, Henderson, NV 89062)

Guardianship occurs when an individual, usually a person (typically) of advanced age) has lost capacity to the point that it is no longer safe for them to make decisions for themselves.

Lost capacity can be for finances, healthcare choices or living choices.

The Guardianship Court can appoint somebody called a Guardian, to essentially step in that person's shoes, and be a guardian for them.

In a guardianship over the person, the guardian makes personal decisions that affect the ward. This can include:

- Making sure the protected person has food, clothing, a safe place to live
- Ensuring the protected person has basic necessities
- Making medical, dental, psychological and other appropriate healthcare decisions for the protected person
- Making sure the protected person receives the right education and training

A guardian over the estate makes decisions about the ward's finances. These decisions can include:

- Deciding how to pay the protected person's bills
- Making sure the protected person's income, savings and finances are protected
- Ensuring appropriate stock and bond sales and transfers and otherwise

*Check within your state, to better understand the laws of that state.

The 7 MUST HAVES

Seven documents you will possibly need to fill out before you die.

1. **Last Will & Testament**

   The fundamental purpose of a Will is to outline who will receive your assets upon your death. Another important purpose of a Will is to specify guardianship for your minor children. A guardian is one who takes legal responsibility for the care of our minor or incapacitated children after you are gone. It is important to understand that a will does not become effective until the date of death. So it does not provide any benefits during your lifetime. A will can be changed at any time (assuming you are not mentally incapacitated). It can be amended by using a codicil or revoked by writing a new will. A will can also create a trust upon your death (more on this below). If your estate is large enough (over $5.49 million in 2017), you may also need to incorporate federal estate tax planning into your documents.

2. **Trust**

   A Trust is a legal instrument that provides ongoing management for your assets. It can be inter vivos (also known as a Living Trust, which exists during your lifetime) or

Testamentary (one that is created by your will upon your death). It is a good idea to leave assets in trust if the beneficiaries are minors, incapacitated, or if they are simply not fiscally responsible. The trust document names a Trustee who has the responsibility of managing the assets in the Trust and determines when and how much of the Trust assets to distribute (subject to the terms you have written in the Trust). You may want to name a trustee while your child is under a certain age, say 25 or 30. Then, once your child reaches that specific age, they can either act as their own Trustee, or the Trust can terminate and distribute all of the assets to your child outright.

3. **Power of Attorney or Advance Directive (in some states)**

A Power of Attorney allows you to empower someone else to act on your behalf for legal, medical and financial decisions. It can be a Durable Power of Attorney, proxy or healthcare agent, which becomes effective immediately, or a Springing Power of Attorney, which becomes effective upon a stipulated event, typically when you are disabled or mentally incompetent. It is critical that you completely trust the person to whom you provide this power, as he or she can legally act on your behalf. You might want to select co-agents, where they serve as equals, or successive agents where the second appointed person will act in the event that the first person cannot. This can be helpful if you choose a spouse or close family member. They may be required to make difficult decisions regarding your care, such as initiation or termination of certain care measures. Please think this through thoroughly.

4. Healthcare Power of Attorney

A Healthcare Power of Attorney (also known as a Medical Power of Attorney) gives a trusted individual the authority to make decisions about your medical treatment should you be unable to do so on your own. No financial authority is granted in this document, only medical power. So you could provide one person the Durable Power of Attorney and another person the Healthcare Power of Attorney if you desire.

5. Living Will

While the Healthcare Power of Attorney authorizes another to make medical decisions on your behalf, a Living Will (also known as a Directive to Physicians) sets out your predetermined wishes regarding end-of-life care should you become terminally ill or permanently unconscious. Essentially it takes the decision to withhold life out of the hands of your medical providers and the ones you love so that they are not burdened by it and so that you can be assured your wishes are respected.

6. HIPAA Release

One of the important provisions of the Health Insurance Portability and Accountability Act of 1996 (HIPPA)is the obligation that medical records be kept confidential. While this is definitely an important requirement, it can have severe unintended consequences. Without the legal authority to share medical records, your family may not be able to obtain important information regarding your medical condition and treatment if you were to become incapacitate. A HIPAA release allows your medical providers to share and discuss your medical situation with whomever you specify in the document.

7. **Letter of Intent**

A Letter of Intent is a simple, non-binding personal letter to the ones you love expressing your desires and special requests. It may include information regarding burial or cremation, or a specific bequest of collectibles or personal items. While it does not typically have legal authority, it can help to clear up confusion regarding your personal preferences.

Estate planning can be complex and the laws vary widely by state. This article is general in nature and is not meant to provide legal advice. I recommend that you engage the services of an estate planning attorney to discuss your wishes and prepare the appropriate documents.

ASK YOURSELF: WHAT ARE MY PERSONAL DESIRES?

1. What do I most value about my physical or mental well-being?
2. What are my thoughts regarding end of life care?

3. Would I want to be sedated if it were necessary to control pain, even if it makes me drowsy or puts me to sleep much of the time? How do I define acceptable pain?

4. Would I want to have a hospice team or palliative care (comfort care) available to me?

5. Would I want to be at home if I am considered terminal or placed in a Nursing facility?

6. Would I want to write a letter to or prepare a recorded message for anyone? Perhaps to be open and read or heard at a future time?

7. How do I want to be remembered? If I write my own epitaph or obituary what would I say?

8. What is my desire? To be cremated or buried?

9. What is my desire? Funeral or memorial service, songs, readings etc.?

10. What is important for others to know about me that only I can share?

These questions and more can be answered by you in the workbook portion of this book. Please complete it and place in a safe place as well as share the location should something happen to you. By answering questions such as above, you can see it can help your loved one at the time of need.

The following are national numbers for organizations that can provide you with more information about getting your affairs in order:

AARP

1-888-687-2277 (toll free)

1-877-434-7598 (TTY/toll-free)

1-877-342-2277 (espanol/linea gratis)

1-866-238-9488 (TTY/Linea gratis)

member@aarp.org

www.aarp.org.health

Caringinfo

National Hospice and Palliative Care Organization

1-800-658-8898 (toll free)

caringinfo@nhpco.org

www.caringinfo.org

Centers for Medicare & Medicaid Services

1-877-486-2048 (TTY/toll-free)

www.medicare.gov

Eldercare Locator

1-800-677-1116 (toll free)

www.eldercare.gov

*Please seek the professional advice of an Estate Planning Attorney, Guardianship, Elder Law Attorney in your local area. Here are a few attorneys in Las Vegas and Indiana areas:

Free Cremation (if offered in your state and if you qualify)

1. Lifescienceanatomical.com – 702-558-0198 Las Vegas, NV
2. Donorcure.com – 1-8000-928-8233
3. Sciencecare.com – 1-800-417-3747

Suggested Estate Planning Attorney's in Henderson, NV, Las Vegas, NV and Lafayette, IN or find one in your local area:

1. A. Collins Hunsaker, Jeffrey Burr Estate Planning & Probate Attorneys, 2600 Paseo Verde Parkway, Ste. 200, Henderson, NV 89074, 702-433-4455

2. Young Law Group, Shane Jasmine Young, 6910 S. Cimarron Road, Ste. 230, Las Vegas, NV 89113 702-473-5600 shane@younglawNV.com

3. Miltina A. Gavia, Attorney at Law, Fehrenback, Taylor Law Office, 12 N. Third Street, Ste. 100, Lafayette, Indiana 47901-0310, 765-420-0714 fehrenbachtaylor.com/miltina

Suggested: Funeral Homes: Las Vegas, NV and Indianapolis, IN or find one in your local area:

1. Serenity Funeral Home, 3435 W. Cheyenne Ave., N. LV 89032 702-647-0123 serenitynv.com

2. Bluitt & Son Funeral Home, Nathan Bluitt, 511 E. Monroe St. Kokomo, IN 46901 - 765-457-3714 meaningfulfunerals.net

3. Lavenia & Summers 5811 E. 38th St. Indianapolis, IN 46218 317-547-5814 laveniasummers.com

"If any of you lacks wisdom, you should ask of God, who gives generously to all without finding fault, and it will be given to you."

- James 1:5 NIV

What to Do "When" Death Occurs | 4

"Then I heard a voice from heaven say, "Write this: Blessed are the dead who die in the Lord from now on."
Revelation 14:13 (NIV)

"Therefore, we do not lose heart. Though outwardly we are wasting away, yet inwardly we are being renewed day by day. For our light and momentary troubles are achieving for us an eternal glory that far outweighs them all. So we fix our eyes not on what is seen, but on what is unseen, since what is seen is temporary, but what is unseen is eternal. "
2 Corinthians 4:16-18 (NIV)

This chapter, by far, may be one of the most difficult ones in this entire book. In addition to grappling with your own feelings and emotions, there are tangible, legal, and financial components that you have to be concerned with. Although this chapter is not exhaustive, it does provide you with a starting place.

Home

When a death occurs at home and your loved one is **not** under hospice care, please call 911 and a police officer will respond to the home and take it from there. If your loved one is under hospice care, please call the hospice nurse first. They will advise from there.

If you have to call the funeral home, the funeral home staff will respond to the location of passing and receive your loved one into their care. They will ask the following questions:

- Caller's name and phone number
- Name of the deceased
- Address and/or directions to the home
- Or name of hospital or Nursing facility

Things to Do:

- Contact close family and/or friends of the deceased
- Contact the deceased doctor (if hospice is not involved)
- If deceased cared for dependent children/grandchildren, make arrangements for their immediate care
- Look for any written instructions/important papers, Will, Insurance Policy, Organ Donor information (possibly on drivers license)

Hospital or Nursing Home

If death occurs in the hospital or nursing home, the nurse or charge nurse will call the funeral home of your choice to pick up your loved one **after** you and family have spent time with them and said your goodbyes. Notify the nurse when you all are ready to leave. They will call the funeral home to pick up your loved one. I strongly recommend you leave the premises before the funeral home picks up your loved one. That is not something you want to see.

The next business day, call the funeral home to schedule an appointment to meet with one of the funeral directors to begin making arrangements to include if you want your loved one to be cremated, have a Memorial Service or a Funeral, setting the date, time and location of funeral whether your choice is for services to be held at Funeral home or church. That is your option. Do not allow the Funeral Director to encourage you to have the service at their facility until you speak to your Pastor's Secretary or Administrative Assistant or your Pastor to see if the church is available.

Ask if you can have the service at your or your loved ones church home which could save money. Also ask if they have accommodations to have the Repass (fellowship meal for family and friends after the funeral) at the church, that could also save you money. Most Pastor's will waive fees to have the service of the deceased at their home church. It is customary to bless the Pastor with an Honorariam of your choice (example: $50-$200) but it is not mandatory. But ask the secretary what services they offer for members and the cost. Prepare yourself, some churches charge to use their church and area for Repass.

I suggest you request the funeral home give you a choice of two dates, for the service, then contact your Pastor or Clergy with those dates to see if and when they are available to conduct the Funeral or Memorial Service. We as a people sometimes will select a date, time and location for the funeral without speaking to the church or its representative, to see if the Pastor is available, then we're upset or disappointed when we don't get that date. Ask Pastor before setting a date.

Funeral home service costs have increased over time for burial and/or cremation. They may offer various packages. It is good to take a trusted family member or friend to the meeting with you. Do not be enticed or coerced into making a decision right away. You will have questions. Write them down and take the questions with you.

Death has no age limit. When we are younger, we feel we don't need to purchase Life Insurance yet because we aren't old. Not true. The death angel is ageless. Death comes to all ages. I share with young adults it's ok to complete the forms I created so your family will know your desires. I promise you that having forms like this will definitely relieve a heavy load or burden off the family. It will still hurt but it will help expedite things.

The moment someone dies, it's as though everything that anyone says to you…..is muted. You can't hear them nor understand them. Your emotions are all over the place. Your heart seems to be pounding out of your chest. You can't breathe. You have a headache, stomachache, tears are flowing profusely. You wonder will they ever stop. It may feel as though someone has stabbed you in the stomach and twisted the knife, it hurts so bad. You're thinking of people you need to be notified, but you don't have the strength; you can't speak clearly without crying and you can't remember phone numbers.

So, what should you do?

It is important that you minimize the franticness of this moment by drawing from a support system that can help you. But, be careful because if you are not prepared, this can be chaotic and confusing.

Take your time, especially if it suddenly feels like everyone wants you to make major decisions. Please select someone close to you to be with you for the next few days or few weeks and ask them to have a notepad and pen or pencil to write down everything you say you need to do or think you might need to do.

Trust me, it helps. Keep that notebook with you at all times or have that person have it with them every time they are with you. Keep it in a certain place so you will know where it is when that person leaves.

Here are examples of some of the questions that you may have about the decisions that need to be made:

- Are you interested in your loved one being an Organ donor? If so, you have 12-36 hours to decide from death to donation.

- Which mortuary have you selected? Most hospitals will give you a few hours to spend with your loved one after death so you can call other family members to come. But after a while they will need you to tell them which mortuary you want to pick up your loved one. Some hospitals have Mortuary's on a rotation list so if you don't know which one you want, they will select one for you. There is a cost for removal of the body from the hospital to the Mortuary.

- If your loved one does not have Life Insurance, most mortuaries have third party loan companies they will recommend you too to pay the funeral costs and you will make monthly installment payments with interest.

- Someone MUST commit to paying for the funeral rather it is through Life Insurance, Cash or loan before they accept the body.

- Note: only a licensed funeral home, hospital or law enforcement can legally move a body.

- I strongly recommend that you, family and friends leave the hospital before the funeral home/mortuary picks up your loved one. That is not something you want to witness.

- If you have not decided Cremation or Burial for your loved one, I guarantee the price will help your decision. The Mortuary needs to know this information very quickly.

- If you are having a viewing and funeral, I recommend having them both in the same day, it is less expensive. Example: Viewing 10a-12p and Funeral start at 12p-2p or less.

- Do you want open casket or closed casket?

- Do you have insurance, if so, what is the name of the company, policy number and their phone number?

- Doctors and hospitals do not notify Social Security of a death, you as next of kin will have to and if you don't, the government can fine you. For widows you can get $225 widow benefit. They will notify Medicare.

- Every bank, insurance company, job, or business your loved one is affiliated with will "demand" a Death Certificate. This can be very costly. So you will need to know how many death certificates you need? Some companies will accept a copy, others will not, so please ask the company or business. You might need 5-10-20. So ask!! And it may take 2-3 weeks to get the Death Certificates and they must be paid for up front before they are ordered or the Mortuary will add the total cost to your bill.

- If your loved one has money in a bank account and you notify the bank of the death in the right way, and your name is on the account you more than likely will not have a problem withdrawing assets, emptying safe deposit boxes and can have the deceased loved one's name removed from the account in ample time. But if you tell the bank the wrong way, all funds are likely to be frozen for months and you will have to get an attorney.

- The Mortuary will offer to create the Obituary and Program and many other amenities for a cost. Be sure to ask what that cost is, before signing on the dotted line.

As you reflect over these questions, do not rush to make a decision. Although some of them are timely and urgent—give yourself as much time as possible. If you rush, you may make some mistakes and you don't want to create any unnecessary guilt or regrets.

Jesus said to her, "I am the resurrection and the life. The one who believes in me will live, even though they die; and whoever lives by believing in me will never die. Do you believe this?"

- John 11:25-26 NIV

How to Talk to Children About Death | 5

"We will not hide them from their descendants; we will tell the next generation the praiseworthy deeds of the Lord, His power, and the wonders He has done."
Psalm 78:4 (NIV)

"Train up a child in the way he should go; even when he is old he will not depart from it."
Proverbs 22:6 (ESV)

"These commandments that I give you today are to be on your hearts. Impress them on your children. Talk about them when you sit at home and when you walk along the road, when you lie down and when you get up."
Deuteronomy 6:6-7 (NIV)

"He heals the brokenhearted and binds up their wounds."
Psalm 147:3 (NIV)

Children have always had a special place in God's eyes. There are numerous scriptures that reflect his profound love and protection of children. As such, I begin this chapter with numerous scriptures because of the special place that children have with God. Whether it is a child, a grandchild, a friend or a distant cousin, it is never easy to discuss death with a child. Developmentally, many of them do not fully grasp the finite nature of death. Some may even think of it as a perpetual state of sleep.

In my experiences as a minister, it's never easy to deal with death, period! As adults, it overwhelms us. And it's even harder for children to move through. Death can occur in many ways. It may be sudden, expected, prolonged or accidental. Part of the experience is finding ways to express what's happened, to make sense of what's happened, and finally to accept what's happened. It is not easy.

Grieving children often feel alone. They think no one understands what they are going through, including God. It seems as though a tape is constantly running through their minds saying, *God doesn't love me, God isn't nice, God doesn't care, my life is ruined, I will never be happy.* Their emotions are all over the place, just like adults. They don't know what to feel or how to feel it properly, if you will.

All they know is someone they love, has died. The reason why God's words should be passed on to children is so that the children may set their hope in God and not forget the works of God.

There should be a continuous overflow of God's Words on our mouths, speaking them over our children and helping them to hide the truths of the Word of God in their hearts. We are Christians and I taught my children to pray and they saw me pray and read the Word of God. We attended bible study and church regularly. I sung in the choir and I was in a Gospel singing group. My children attended rehearsals with me so they could also hear the Word through song.

As I mentioned, when my first husband died, our baby girl was two years old. She loved her Daddy and he affectionately nicknamed her "Peanut". After he passed, she would periodically ask for her Daddy in the morning and when she thought he would come home from work. Or she would look out the window and see his truck and say "Daddy, Daddy". I would tell her sometimes with tears streaming down my face, Daddy is in heaven baby and one day you will see him. She began to lift her hands and say, "Hallelujah, Hallelujah" which is something our children saw me do and say many times.

The day came for the viewing (or wake). I was very concerned as to how she would act when seeing him in a casket so I decided to only take her to the viewing because I felt she would get restless at a two-hour funeral. Even though she could walk, I decided to carry her in. I began to pray asking God for strength to let us get through this moment. I had no idea how our baby would respond seeing her Daddy whom she loved in a casket.

When we walked in family and friends who were there became almost silent when they saw her in my arms. You could hear sniffles as people were crying and soft whispers of "bless her heart". We approached the casket and our baby daughter looked down at her Daddy and said, "Daddy sleeping with Jesus".

Can you imagine how I felt at that moment? Here, my baby daughter understood what many adults struggle with. And the adults who bore witness to her words responded accordingly. God is my witness, that place went into Praise. We all gave God the Glory for allowing our baby to know where her Daddy was. Now that doesn't mean all children will have that experience, but I taught my children about

Jesus and talked to them about death. We as parents can never be sure they totally understand but we must pray and ask God for His help and trust that He will do it. He says in Philippians 4:19, But my God shall supply all my needs according to His riches and Glory by Christ Jesus. God did supply my need and he answered my prayer.

Here are some suggestions for you to **"DO"**:

1. Love them right where they are. Tell the truth about what happened right away. The truth gives an explanation for your tears and pain. Being open and emotional can help your child learn how to mourn.

2. Be prepared for a variety of emotional responses. Realize that however you approach this subject, your child will be upset, and perhaps, even angry at the loss. Accept your child's emotional reactions. You will have time to address things again after your child's had time to process the initial trauma.

3. Make sure to use the words dead or died. Many find using the words dead or died uncomfortable – and prefer using phrases like, passed away, lost, crossed over, went to sleep - but research shows that using realistic words to describe death helps the grieving process.

4. Share information in doses. Gauge what your child can handle by giving information in small bits at a time. You'll know what more to do based on the questions your child asks.

5. Be comfortable saying, "I don't know." Having all the answers is never easy, especially during a time of such heartache. It's helpful to tell your child that you may not know about certain things, like, "How did grandma die?" "What happens to Aunt Betty at the funeral home," "What made Skip run into the street, Mommy?" or other unanswerable questions.

6. Cry. Cry together. Cry often. It's healthy and healing.

7. Allow your child to participate in rituals. Let children assist in picking clothing for your loved one, photos to use for the service, a song or spiritual reading. This will help them gain a sense of control of the traumatic loss.

8. Let your child grieve in his or her own way. Allow your child to be silent about the death. It's also natural for a child to feel lonely and isolate themselves at this time too. It's also common for children to seem unaffected by the loss. There is no right way to grieve.

9. Prepare your child for what they will see in the funeral home or service, who will be there, how people may be feeling and what they will be doing. For young children, be specific in your descriptions of what the surroundings will look like. For example, describe the casket and clothes and that the body will be laying down in a posed position. Or if it's a memorial service, talk about where the body is, if it's been cremated, in a closed coffin or already buried. Bring along someone to care for the child if you are distraught.

10. Prepare your child for the future without your loved one. Talk about how it will feel to celebrate birthdays, anniversaries, holidays, and special moments without your loved one. Ask your child to help plan how to move through the next calendar event.

11. Prepare to talk about thoughts and feelings often. It is likely that you'll have to tend to the subject of death for days, weeks and months to come. Check in and be available for ongoing discussions since mourning is a process.

12. Remember to take care of yourself. As parents, we sometimes forget about taking care of ourselves during this time. Children learn from what they see, so be a role model for self-care at this critical time.

13. Seek a professional counselor if need be for yourself and your child/children.

14. Love your children right where they are.

15. Share with them no one is completely gone as long as they can remember their loved one in their heart. Remember their smile, laughter, fragrance, how much they loved them, fun things about them and look at photos that make you happy.

Here are some: **DON'T'S:**

1. Don't hide your grief from your child. Seeing you grieve during and long after your loved one's death will let the

child know that it's normal and healthy to cry and fee sad after a significant loss.

2. Don't be afraid to share memories of your loved one. Sometimes parents feel afraid to talk about the person who has died, thinking it will cause pain to others. Research shows that the pain of re-living memories or sharing stories actually aids in healing and closure.

3. Don't avoid connecting with your child because you feel helpless or uncomfortable, or don't know what to say. Sometimes a knowing look can be a powerful connection. Even a touch or a hug can offer great comfort.

4. Don't change the subject when your child comes into the room. Doing so places a mark of taboo on the subject of death. Instead, adjust your wording and level of information when a child is present.

5. Don't change your daily routine. Children need consistency. Try as much as possible to keep your usual daily routines at home and at work. Also, try to ensure that your child continues to take part in their usual activities like school and social events.

6. Don't think that death puts a ban on laughter. Laughter is a great healing tool. Being able to laugh about memories or moments with your loved one signals just how important their presence was in your life.

7. Don't put a time limit on your child's bereavement-or your own. Everyone grieves in their own way. Recognize that a new normal will have to occur – and that time is needed to

readjust to a significant death. If you need additional support, reach out to your child's school, physician, or religious community. Professional help with a grief counselor, mental health therapist or others trained in bereavement can be sought as well.

"Let the little children come to me, and do not hinder them, for the kingdom of heaven belongs to such as these."

-- Matthew 19:14 NIV

Organizing Your Information | 6

This chapter will provide you with practical information, including templates that you can copy, or alter to best suit your needs. Keep in mind that each template is intended to serve as a guide. Be sure to consult with other family members, your spiritual advisor and pastor as some denominations have very specific guidelines about the order of a funeral/homegoing, memorial or graveside service.

Whenever possible, try to get as much information from your loved one before he/she becomes ill. It is also highly recommended that you fill these out so that your loved ones know what you desire. Also keep in mind that having this discussion may be very difficult. Writing an obituary is an overt reminder of death. Be sure to take your time and give yourself time to reflect—for some, this will lead to regret while for others preparing your own obituary will serve as a rich reminder of a life well lived. If doing these forms alone is not beneficial then ask someone who you truly trust to assist you or serve as a sounding board for your ideas and thoughts.

FORM A

MY DESIRES/WISHES:

SUGGESTION: PLACE THIS COMPLETED FORM, PHOTOS AND ALL IMPORTANT INFORMATION IN AN ENVELOPE. THEN PLACE IN PORTFOLIO, PLACE IN A SECURE PLACE AND LET YOUR LOVED ONE KNOW WHERE IT CAN BE FOUND. OR PLACE IN SOMETHING AS SIMPLE AS A GALLON SIZE OR LARGER ZIP-LOCK FREEZER BAG(S) AND PLACE IN YOUR FREEZER OR OTHER SPECIFIC LOCATION YOU SPECIFY. TELL YOUR FAMILY WHERE IT CAN BE FOUND IN CASE OF EMERGENCY.

DATE: _____

MY FULL NAME:

_____

MY ADDRESS CITY, STATE & ZIP:

_____

_____

DATE OF BIRTH:

_____

CURRENT AGE:

_____

I AM: AN "ORGAN DONOR"   **NOT** AN "ORGAN DONOR"
(PLEASE CIRCLE ONE)
- I PLACED A COPY OF MY DRIVER'S LICENSE OR STATE I.D. WITH THESE RECORDS.
  YES OR NO
- I PLACED A COPY OF MY SOCIAL SECURITY CARD WITH THESE RECORDS
  YES OR NO

- I PLACED A COPY OF MY INSURANCE POLICY WITH THESE RECORDS
  YES   OR   NO

I AM: DIVORCED   SINGLE   MARRIED   WIDOWED
SEPARATED   (PLEASE CIRCLE ONE)

NAME OF SPOUSE:

_____

PHONE NUMBER:

_____

NAME OF PARENTS: LIVING OR DECEASED:

_____

_____

_____

PERSON(S) TO CALL IN CASE OF EMERGENCY & PHONE NUMBER:

_____

_____

_____

RELATIONSHIP?

_____

HOW MANY CHILDREN TOTAL? _____   LIVING? _____
DECEASED? _____

FULL NAMES, ADDRESSES AND PHONE NUMBERS: (IF YOU NEED
MORE SPACE TO WRITE, PLEASE WRITE ON THE BACK OF THIS
PAGE OR ATTACH ANOTHER SHEET OF PAPER.

_____

_____

_____

_____

_____

_____

_____

_____

_____

I AM EMPLOYED WITH: NAME, ADDRESS & PHONE NUMBER OF EMPLOYER:

_____

_____

_____

I AM RETIRED:　　　　YES OR NO　　　　(PLEASE CIRCLE ONE)
I RETIRED FROM:

_____

_____

_____

PHONE: _____

1. I APPOINT (FULL NAME):

    _____

    _____

    TO OVERSEE MY FUNERAL AND HANDLE MY AFFAIRS.

2. ADDRESS:

    _____

    _____

3. CITY, STATE & ZIP:

    _____

    _____

4. PHONE# H- (   )_____
    CELL #: (   ) _____

5. I DO   OR   DO NOT   HAVE LIFE INSURANCE (PLEASE CIRCLE ONE).

6. NAME OF MY LIFE INSURANCE COMPANY AND PHONE NUMBER IS:

    _____

7. MY POLICY NUMBER IS:

    _____

8. MY LIFE INSURANCE POLICY LOCATION IS: (IF NOT IN PORFOLIO OR FREEZER BAG)

    _____
    _____
    _____
    _____

    I HAVE A PRE-PAID FUNERAL PLAN/POLICY WITH: (NAME, ADDRESS AND PHONE NUMBER OF FUNERAL HOME)?

    _____
    _____
    _____

9. NAME OF CEMETERY?

    _____

10. PLOT NUMBER (IF KNOWN)

    _____

11. MY PRE-PAID FUNERAL POLICY AMOUNT IS $_____
    AND IT IS PAID IN FULL. ....OR

12. MY PRE-PAID FUNERAL POLICY AMOUNT I HAVE PAID INTO IT, IS?
    $_____

13. BALANCE OWED ON MY PRE-PAID POLICY IN THE AMOUNT OF:
    $_____

14. I HAVE A CHECKING ACCOUNT WITH: (NAME, ADDRESS & PHONE # OF BANK):

_____
_____
_____
_____

15. NAME(S) ON CHECKING ACCOUNT:

_____
_____
_____

16. MY CHECKING ACCOUNT ROUTING NUMBER IS:

_____

(IT IS THE FIRST 9 NUMBERS BOTTOM LEFT ON CHECK)

17. MY CHECKING ACCOUNT NUMBER IS:

_____

(IT IS 12 MIDDLE NUMBERS AT BOTTOM OF CHECK)

18. I HAVE A SAVINGS ACCOUNT WITH (NAME OF BANK):

_____

19. MY SAVINGS ACCOUNT NUMBER IS:

_____

20. I HAVE A SAFE DEPOSIT BOX AT (NAME & ADDRESS OF BANK) BOX
NUMBER AND LOCATION OF KEY?

_____
_____
_____
_____
_____

21. I HAVE A 401κ OR OTHER ACCOUNTS WITH (NAME, LOCATION AND
ACCOUNT NUMBERS):

_____
_____
_____
_____
_____

22. MY SOCIAL SECURITY NUMBER IS:

_____

23. (OPTIONAL) MY ATTORNEYS NAME, ADDRESS AND PHONE NUMBER IS:

_____

_____

_____

24. I WANT TO BE   CREMATED   BURIED OR   IN A MAUSOLEUM
    (PLEASE CIRCLE ONE)

25. IF BURIED: I WANT VIEWING AND OPEN CASKET FUNERAL ALL IN SAME
    DAY?
    YES   OR   NO   (PLEASE CIRCLE ONE).

26. I WANT MY VIEWING ONE DAY AND FUNERAL THE NEXT DAY?   YES   OR
    NO   (PLEASE CIRCLE ONE).

27. IF BURIED: I WANT VIEWING AND CLOSED CASKET FUNERAL ALL IN SAME
    DAY?

    YES   OR NO   (PLEASE CIRCLE ONE).

28. I WANT MY CASKET CLOSED DURING VIEWING AND ENTIRE SERVICE?
    YES OR NO   (PLEASE CIRCLE ONE).

29. I WANT TO BE CREMATED AND HAVE A MEMORIAL SERVICE A DAY THAT
    IS COMFORTABLE FOR FAMILY AFTER CREMATION: YES   OR   NO
    (PLEASE CIRCLE ONE).

30. IF CREMATED: WHAT DO YOU WANT DONE WITH YOUR ASHES?

_____

_____

_____

31. IF YOU WANT YOUR BODY SHIPPED TO ANOTHER STATE, PLEASE LIST
     NAME, ADDRESS, CITY & STATE AND PHONE NUMBER OF FUNERAL HOME
     TO RECEIVE YOUR BODY?

_____

_____

_____

_____

32. NAME, ADDRESS, PHONE NUMBER OF CEMETERY FOR BURIAL:

_____

_____

_____

_____

33. WHAT COLOR CASKET:

_____

34. WHAT KIND OF FLOWERS FOR CASKET SPRAY (IT LAYS ON TOP BOTTOM HALF OF CASKET)?

_____

_____

_____

_____

35. PHOTO I WANT ON THE FRONT OF PROGRAM IS IN "MY DESIRES PACKET": (LOCATION & DESCRIBE PICTURE)

_____

_____

36. POEM I WANT ON BACK OF MY PROGRAM IS IN "MY DESIRES PACKET" OR ATTACHED TO THIS FORM.

37. 10 PICTURES (YOU MAY ADD MORE) I WANT IN THE PROGRAM CAN BE FOUND IN "MY DESIRES PACKET" OR (LOCATION)

_____

_____

_____

_____

38. I WANT TO WEAR: COLOR/STYLE OF DRESS OR SUIT AND WHERE THESE ITEMS CAN BE FOUND?

_____

_____

_____

39. SHOES OR SOCKS/FOOTIES, IF DESIRED BUT NOT NEEDED

_____

_____

40. JEWELRY:
_____
_____

41. UNDERCLOTHES: (UNDERSHIRT, BOXERS/BRIEFS, SOCKS/FOOTIES, BRA, PANTIES, UNDER SLIP, (OPTIONAL) CAN BE FOUND:
_____
_____
_____
_____

42. MY HAIRSTYLIST OR BARBERS NAME AND PHONE NUMBER IS:
_____
_____

43. MY MAKE-UP ARTIST NAME AND PHONE NUMBER IS:
_____
_____

44. THE COLOR I WANT MY NAIL POLISHED IS:
_____OR IF MY HANDS ARE NOT PRESENTABLE, PLEASE PURCHASE GLOVES FOR ME TO WEAR.

45. NAME & PHONE # OF PASTOR, RABBI OR PRIEST TO CONDUCT EULOGY IS:
_____
_____
_____
_____

46. NAME & PHONE NUMBER OF PERSON TO SING?
_____
_____

47. SCRIPTURE(S) I WANT READ:
OLD TESTAMENT: _____
NEW TESTAMENT: _____

48. NAME & ARTIST OF 1ST SONG TO BE SUNG:

_____

_____

49. NAME & ARTIST OF 2ND SONG (OPTIONAL) TO BE SUNG:

_____

_____

50. REPASS DINNER (THIS IS FELLOWSHIP DINNER AFTER SERVICE) CONTACT PERSONS INFORMATION & LOCATION?_____

_____

_____

(OPTIONAL) SUGGESTED REPASS DINNER DESIRED MENU:

LIST OF NAMES OF PHONE NUMBERS OF FAMILY AND FRIENDS TO BE NOTIFIED OF MY DEATH:

IF ADDITIONAL SPACE IS NEEDED WRITE ON THE BACK OF THIS PAGE OR ADD ADDITIONAL SHEET OF PAPER.

ATTACH A POEM OR SCRIPTURE READING TO PLACE ON BACK
PAGE OF PROGRAM:

*IF YOU NEED MORE SPACE TO WRITE, PLEASE USE THE BACK OF
PAGE(S):

BACK OF PROGRAM

(POEM)

FORM B

INFORMATIONAL OBITUARY TEMPLATE

PRINT - FULL NAME OF DECEASED:

_____

_____

DATE OF BIRTH: MONTH, DAY & YEAR:

_____

_____

BIRTHPLACE (CITY & STATE):

_____

_____

CITY & STATE DECEASED WAS BORN IN:

_____

_____

CITY & STATE DECEASED WAS RAISED IN:

_____

_____

MOTHER'S FULL NAME:

_____

MAIDEN NAME:_____

FATHER'S FULL NAME:

_____

SPOUSE (WIFE) MAIDEN NAME BEFORE MARRIAGE:

_____

DATE OF MARRIAGE: _____

LOCATION OF MARRIAGE:

_____

_____

NAME OF HIGH SCHOOL, CITY & STATE DECEASED ATTENDED:

_____

GRADUATED: YES OR NO (PLEASE CIRCLE ONE).

NAME OF COLLEGE ATTENDED:

_____

GRADUATED: YES OR NO   (PLEASE CIRCLE ONE).
NAME OF COLLEGE DEGREE:

_____

MILITARY?   YES OR NO (PLEASE CIRCLE ONE).
IF YES, WHAT BRANCH: _____
WHERE DID HE/SHE SERVE? _____
HOW MANY YEAR(S) DID HE/SHE SERVE_____
RANK: _____
WHAT WAR(S) DID THEY SERVE IN:

_____

_____

WHERE WAS DECEASED EMPLOYED:

_____

LENGTH OF TIME: _____
WAS DECEASED RETIRED: YES OR NO (PLEASE CIRCLE ONE).
IF SO, RETIRED FROM WHERE:

_____

_____

NAME OF CHURCH

_____

_____

NAME OF PASTOR:

_____

_____

MINISTRIES, VOLUNTEER, ACTIVE COMMUNITY INVOLVEMENT OR
SPECIAL ACCOMPLISHMENTS:

_____

_____

_____

_____

_____

HOW MANY SIBLING(S): _____

HOW MANY DECEASED SIBLING(S):_____

NAME OF DECEASED SIBLING(S):

_____

_____

_____

_____

NAMES OF LIVING SIBLINGS:

_____

_____

_____

_____

LIVING CHILDREN: HOW MANY? _____

NUMBER OF DECEASED CHILDREN:_____

WHEN LISTING CHILDREN'S NAMES BELOW, PLEASE INDICATE *IF
DECEASED.

FULL NAME(S) OF CHILDREN & FIRST NAME ONLY OF SPOUSE
PLACED IN PARENTHESIS:

_____

_____

_____

_____

_____

_____

_____

DID HE/SHE GIVE THEIR LIFE TO CHRIST AT AN EARLY AGE: YES OR NO (PLEASE CIRCLE ONE).

HOW MANY GRANDCHILDREN_____
HOW MANY GREAT-GRANDCHILDREN? _____

LIST GRANDCHILDREN(S) FIRST NAME ONLY (OPTIONAL 10 OR LESS)

_____
_____
_____
_____
_____
_____
_____

HOBBIES:
_____
_____

SPORTS:
_____
_____

FRATERNITY OR SORORITY:
_____
_____
_____

ORGANIZATION/CLUBS:
_____
_____
_____

LOCATION OF DEATH: (OPTIONAL) EXAMPLE: HOSPITAL OR
HOME_____

SURVIVOR(S): EXAMPLE: (HE/SHE LEAVES TO CHERISH HIS/HER
MEMORY) FIRST NAME: SPOUSE, PARENTS, SIBLINGS,
CHILDREN/SPOUSE, GRANDCHILDREN AND A HOST OF RELATIVES
AND FRIENDS.

_____
_____
_____
_____
_____
_____
_____
_____

LIST 6 CASKET BEARERS/PALLBEARERS FIRST & LAST NAMES
(THEY CARRY THE CASKET):

_____
_____
_____
_____
_____

OPTIONAL: LIST 4 HONORARY CASKET BEARERS/PALLBEARERS:

_____
_____
_____
_____

LIST 4 FLOWER BEARERS FIRST AND LAST NAMES (THEY CARRY
FLOWERS):

_____
_____
_____
_____

ORDER OF SERVICE EXAMPLE ONE

OFFICIANT NAME: _____

NAME OF CHURCH: _____

EMCEE NAME: (OPTIONAL):_____

PROCESSIONAL (OPTIONAL)...SOFT MUSIC PLAYED WHILE FAMILY AND CLERGY ENTER

OPENING PRAYER...MIN./REV. BRO/SIS. (1ST AND LAST NAME OF PERSON PRAYING)

SCRIPTURE(S)...............................NAME OF MINISTER(S) READING ONE OLD TESTAMENT AND/OR NEW TESTAMENT SCRIPTURE

MUSICAL SELECTION OR SOLO... FIRST AND LAST NAME OF PERSON SINGING

ACKNOWLEDGEMENT & CONDOLENCES...FIRST AND LAST NAME OF PERSON READING

WORDS AND SENTIMENTS: (OPTIONAL) SHORT LIST (2-4 PEOPLE) SPECIFIC MEMBERS OF FAMILY OR FRIENDS TO SPEAK (2 MINUTES PLEASE)

MUSICAL SELECTION OR SOLO... FIRST AND LAST NAME OF PERSON SINGING

EULOGY... TITLE, FIRST AND LAST NAME OF PASTOR/MINISTER AND NAME OF THEIR CHURCH

PARTING VIEW (OPTIONAL)... ....SOFT MUSIC BEING PLAYED

RECESSIONAL:... ....… FAMILY EXIT BEHIND THE CASKET, THEN GUESTS

OPTIONAL EXAMPLE: BURIAL:
SOUTHERN NEVADA VETERANS MEMORIAL CEMETERY
1900 VETERANS MEMORIAL DR.
BOULDER CITY, NV 89005
TIME: 12:00 P.M. (PROMPTLY)

REPASS
LOCATION/ADDRESS/TIME

FORM C
SAMPLE OBITUARY TEMPLATE

CELEBRATION OF LIFE
FOR

(NAME OF DECEASED)

SUNRISE: (DATE OF BIRTH)   SUNSET: (DATE OF DEATH)
(DAY, MONTH, DATE & YEAR OF SERVICE)
(TIME OF SERVICE)

(PHOTO)

(CHURCH OR FUNERAL HOME NAME WHERE SERVICE WILL BE HELD)
(ADDRESS, CITY, STATE, ZIP WHERE SERVICE WILL BE HELD)
NAME OF PASTOR OR OFFICIANT

OBITUARY

ACKNOWLEDGEMENTS

OUR FAMILY WISHES TO ACKNOWLEDGE WITH SINCERE APPRECIATION THE MANY EXPRESSIONS OF LOVE, PRAYER, FOOD AND KINDNESS SHOWN TO US DURING OUR TIME OF BEREAVEMENT. THANK YOU ALL. PLEASE CONTINUE TO PRAY FOR OUR FAMILY. GOD BLESS EACH OF YOU.

HUMBLY SUBMITTED:

ORDER OF SERVICE EXAMPLE TWO

THE FAMILY OF:
(NAME OF DECEASED)
ORDER OF SERVICE
EMCEE NAME
PASTOR'S NAME
NAME OF CHURCH, ADDRESS, CITY, STATE, ZIP
PHONE NUMBER
(*PLEASE PLACE ALL CELL PHONES & ELECTRONIC DEVICES ON MUTE,
VIBRATE OR OFF, THANK YOU)

PROCESSIONAL (OPTIONAL)... ... ...

OPENING PRAYER... ... ...… ... ...

SCRIPTURE(S)... ... ...

MUSICAL SELECTION... ... ...

CONDOLENCES & OBITUARY READ... ... ...

VIDEO/SLIDE SHOW (OPTIONAL)... ... ...

FAMILY REMARKS... ... ... 2 MINUTES PLEASE

MUSICAL SELECTION... ... ...

WORDS OF COMFORT... ... ...…... ... ...…...

INVITATION TO DISCIPLESHIP (OPTIONAL)... ... ...

PARTING VIEW (OPTIONAL)... ... ...

CLOSING PRAYER OR BENEDICTION... ... ...

RECESSIONAL (OPTIONAL)... ... ...
*REPASS:
LOCATION, NAME, ADDRESS, ZIP, TIME

PHOTOS (OPTIONAL)

CERTIFICATE OF ACKNOWLEGEMENT OF NOTARY PUBLIC

STATE OF _____)

COUNTY OF _____)

ON THIS _____ DAY OF _____ 20_____,

BEFORE ME, THE UNDERSIGNED, A NOTARY PUBLIC IN AND FOR SAID

COUNTY OF _____, STATE OF _____,

PERSONALLY APPEARD _____

PERSONALLY KNOWN TO ME (OR PROVED TO ME ON THE BASIS OF

SATISFACTORY EVIDENCE) TO BE THE PERSON WHOSE NAME IS

SUBSCRIBED TO THE WITHIN INSTRUMENT AND ACKNOWLEDGED TO ME

THAT HE OR SHE (PLEASE CIRCLE ONE) EXECUTED THE SAME IN HIS OR

HER AUTORIZED CAPACITY, AND THAT BY HIS OR HER SIGNATURE ON THE

INSTRUMENT, THE PERSON, OR THE ENTITY UPON BEHALD OF WHICH THE

PERSON ACTED, EXECUTED THE INSTRUMENT.

WITNESS MY HAND AND OFFICIAL SEAL

_____

NOTARY PUBLIC

Epilogue

"For everything, there is a season."

As our time together comes to an end, I want to encourage you that thinking about and preparing for death is something that we all need to do. We also need to openly and honestly discuss death with those whom we love. The reality is that losing someone you love can be very devastating, regardless of who you are or how old you are. It happens to everyone and does not discriminate. Just a quick glance in the obituaries of your local paper will help to illuminate this.

Please know that you are not alone and every reader is in my prayers. It doesn't matter if you are a Christian or not, we all go through very similar emotions. For me, as a Christian, it was my faith, my Pastor, my children, friends and family who helped me through one of the most difficult times in my life. Every morning, I would pray, turn on my Christian music and allow it to minister to me. I would sing songs of zion.

I would worship the Lord with tears running down my cheeks but they were tears of joy because I felt His presence. I still sing, read my Word and read daily devotions to encourage myself. Isaiah 41:10 says: "Fear not, for I am with you; be not dismayed, for I am your God; I will strengthen you, I will help you. I will uphold you with my righteous right hand." Turn to this and other scriptures during your time of need.

Also, don't feel as if you must "get over grieving" within a certain amount of time. There are awesome grief counselors, pastors, rabbis, priests and chaplains who are willing to help you through this in the area in which you reside. As an extension of my ministry, I have spoken at various conferences and workshops to encourage and love on those who have suffered loss. I am also a Facilitor for the *Look Good Feel Better Program* through the American Cancer Society where I often teach women how to put on make up, make creative head wraps out of cotton t-shirts or how to wrap scarves very stylish. I have done and still do grief counseling, officiate and sing.

And now, I am blessed to be a vessel for this book. I feel God called me to encourage and love you through the reading of this book, His children, my sister and my brother. NIV, Acts 10:34, "Then Peter began to speak, 'I now realize how true it is that God does not show favoritism.'"; what He did for me, He can do for you. Please know you are not reading these books by happenstance. "The steps of a good man are ordered by the Lord and he delighteth in his way" (Psalm 37:23). Take advantage of the opportunity NOW to get your business in order. If you are reading this book, God is saying to you, ***It's Preparation Time!***

You are welcome to reach out to me, via email if you would like to book me to speak at your church, hospital, hospice, nursing facilities, medical schools, police department, fire department, schools, retirement communities, conferences and workshops. I would be honored!

If any of you have a loved one in transition or have loss a loved one, please accept my sincere condolences. Know that I am praying for God to empower you with His love, presence, strength, comfort and closure. God bless each of you and thank you for reading my book. May the Lord bless you and keep you. The Lord make His face shine upon you and be gracious to you; The Lord lift up His countenance upon you and give you peace.

I look forward to meeting you and giving you a hug.

Bless You,

Minister Cheryl Hall McElroy

"Rejoice always, pray continually, give thanks in all circumstances; for this is God's will for you in Christ Jesus."

-1 Thessalonians 5:16–18 NIV

About the Author

Cheryl Hall McElroy is a woman of God and servant-leader who loves the Lord. She is a child of God who loves singing praises to His name and giving Him glory, honor, and praise. She is a daughter, wife, mother, sister, cousin, grandmother, great-grandmother, friend, ordained minister, licensed hospital chaplain, licensed cosmetologist and licensed cosmetology instructor. A multi-gifted and talented woman who gives from her heart, she has the gift of helping and serving others. Her studies include Clinical Pastoral Education (CPE), Psychology, & Biblical studies.

For bookings, please contact: **cherylhallmcelroy@gmail.com**